FRIENDSHIP BRACELETS!

A SHOW-HOW GUIDE!

Written & illustrated
by Keith Zoo

ODD DOT • NEW YORK

Hey there!

This **Show-How** gives you the know-how on friendship bracelets. We've included only the essentials so you can easily master the FUN-damentals. You'll be sporting and sharing some sweet bracelets in no time. Ready? Let's go!

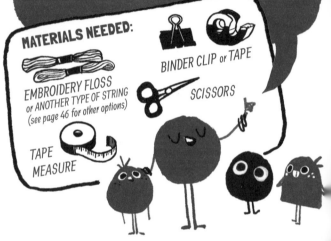

MATERIALS NEEDED:

EMBROIDERY FLOSS
or ANOTHER TYPE OF STRING
(see page 46 for other options)

BINDER CLIP or TAPE

SCISSORS

TAPE MEASURE

TABLE OF CONTENTS

KNOTS to KNOW:

Practice the Macramé (page 4) and Zipper (page 8) bracelets to master these!

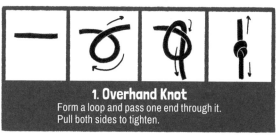

1. Overhand Knot
Form a loop and pass one end through it.
Pull both sides to tighten.

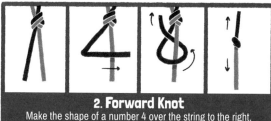

2. Forward Knot
Make the shape of a number 4 over the string to the right.
Pass the working end underneath and up through the
center of the 4. Pull up and to the right to tighten.

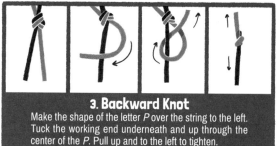

3. Backward Knot
Make the shape of the letter *P* over the string to the left.
Tuck the working end underneath and up through the
center of the *P*. Pull up and to the left to tighten.

HOW TO FINISH YOUR BRACELETS:
Once your bracelet has reached the desired length, it's time to tie it off. This
prevents your bracelet from falling apart. Follow the instructions below.

1. Gather loose strings at the end and tie a tight overhand knot as
   close to the last stitch as possible.
2. Tie the ends together in an overhand knot to finish the bracelet.
   (You might need help with this if you want to tie it on your own wrist!)
3. Cut loose ends.

1
MACRAMÉ

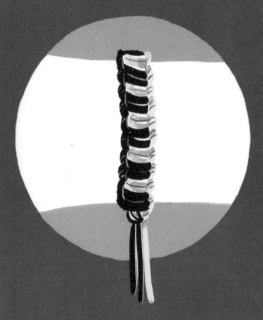

WORKS BEST WITH:
Embroidery Floss, Yarn, Hemp

GATHER:
Two colors (two strings of each for four total)
Measure and cut each string to 24–30 inches

1

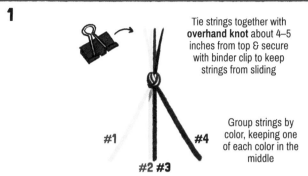

Tie strings together with **overhand knot** about 4–5 inches from top & secure with binder clip to keep strings from sliding

Group strings by color, keeping one of each color in the middle

#1 #4

#2 #3

2

Make **forward knot** as shown with string #1

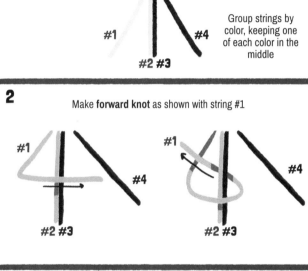

#1 #4

#2 #3

#1 #4

#2 #3

3

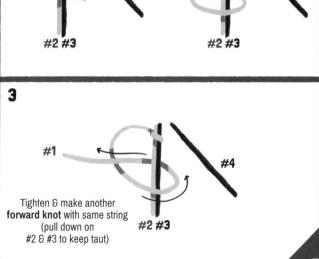

#1 #4

Tighten & make another **forward knot** with same string (pull down on #2 & #3 to keep taut)

#2 #3

#1

#2 #3

#4

Tighten string #1 & switch sides

5

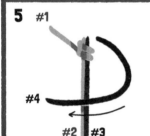

#1

#4

#2 #3

#1

#4

#2 #3

Make **backward knot** as shown with string #4

6

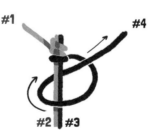

#1

#4

#2 #3

Tighten & make another **backward knot** with same string (pull down on #2 & #3 to keep taut)

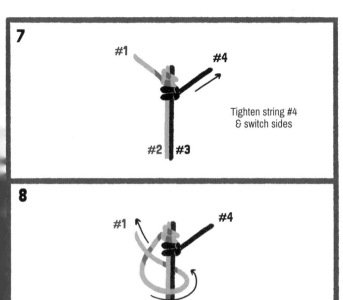

7

#1 #4

#2 #3

Tighten string #4 & switch sides

8

#1 #4

#2 #3

Repeat steps 2–7 until your bracelet is long enough

Follow steps from page 3 to finish!

TIP!

Use a tape measure to measure your wrist. Then you'll know how long to make it!

2

ZIPPER

WORKS BEST WITH:
Embroidery Floss, Yarn, Hemp

GATHER:
Two colors (three strings of each for six total)
Measure and cut each string to 24–30 inches

1

Tie strings together with **overhand knot** about 4–5 inches from top & secure with binder clip to keep strings from sliding

Group strings by color, keeping one of each in the middle

Put aside group #3

#1

#2

#3

2

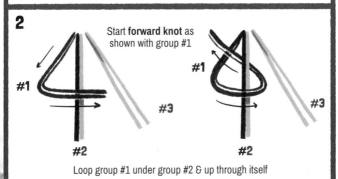

Start **forward knot** as shown with group #1

#1

#2

#3

#1

#2

#3

Loop group #1 under group #2 & up through itself

3

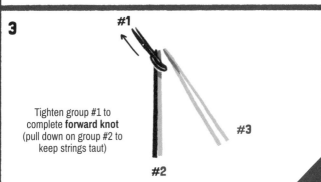

#1

Tighten group #1 to complete **forward knot** (pull down on group #2 to keep strings taut)

#2

#3

4

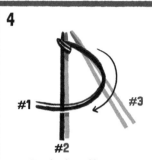

Start **backward knot** as shown with group #1

5

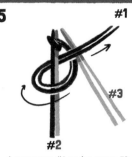

Loop group #1 under group #2 & up through itself

6

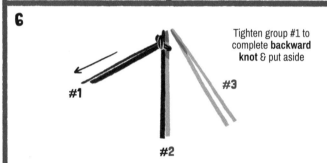

Tighten group #1 to complete **backward knot** & put aside

7

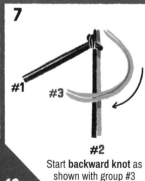

Start **backward knot** as shown with group #3

Loop group #3 under group #2 & up through itself

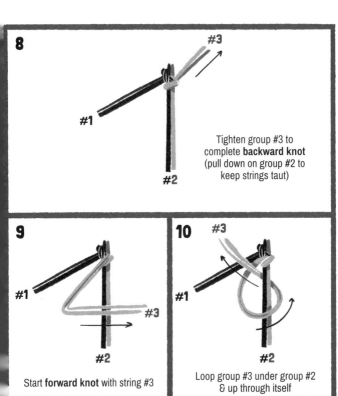

8

#3

#1

#2

Tighten group #3 to complete **backward knot** (pull down on group #2 to keep strings taut)

9

#1

#3

#2

Start **forward knot** with string #3

10

#3

#1

#2

Loop group #3 under group #2 & up through itself

11

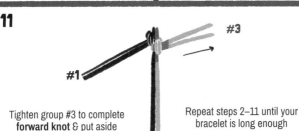

#3

#1

#2

Tighten group #3 to complete **forward knot** & put aside (pull down on group #2 to keep strings taut)

Repeat steps 2–11 until your bracelet is long enough

Follow steps from page 3 to finish!

3

TWIST

WORKS BEST WITH:
Embroidery Floss, Yarn, Hemp

GATHER:
Two colors (two strings of each for four total)
Measure and cut each string to 24–30 inches

1

Tie strings together with **overhand knot** about 4–5 inches from top & secure with binder clip to keep strings from sliding

Group strings by color, keeping one of each color in middle

(Secure bottom of #2 & #3 to keep taut)

#1

#2   #3   #4

2

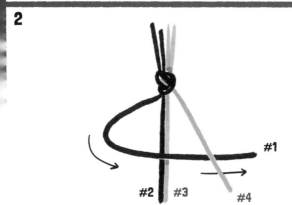

#1

#2   #3   #4

Weave string #1 as shown (over strings #2 & #3 & under string #4)

13

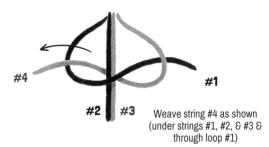

Weave string #4 as shown (under strings #1, #2, & #3 & through loop #1)

4

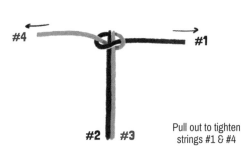

Pull out to tighten strings #1 & #4

5

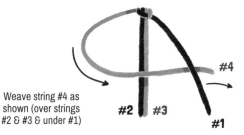

Weave string #4 as shown (over strings #2 & #3 & under #1)

6

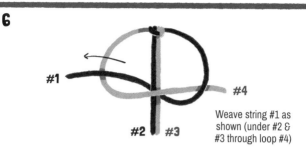

Weave string #1 as shown (under #2 & #3 through loop #4)

7

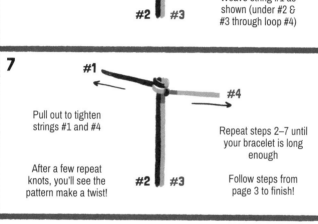

Pull out to tighten strings #1 and #4

After a few repeat knots, you'll see the pattern make a twist!

Repeat steps 2–7 until your bracelet is long enough

Follow steps from page 3 to finish!

Phew! That's a lotta knots!

4

WRAP

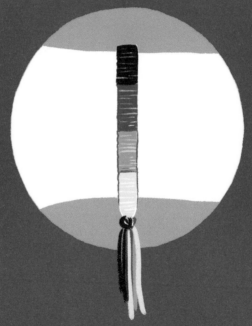

WORKS BEST WITH:
Embroidery Floss, Yarn

GATHER:
Four colors (two strings of each for eight total)
Measure and cut each string to 24–30 inches

1

Tie strings together with **overhand knot** 4–5 inches from top & secure with binder clip to keep strings from sliding

#1

#2   #3   #4

Group strings by color

2

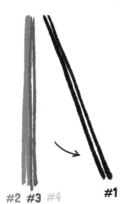

#2 #3 #4   #1

Separate group #1 & pull other strings taut together

3

#2 #3 #4   #1

Loop group #1 around other strings about six times or until you reach desired length

4

Add group #1 to other strings
& separate group #2

#3
#4 #1

#2

5

Loop group #2 around other
strings about 6 times or until
you reach desired length

#3
#4 #1

#2

6

#4 #1 #2

#3

Add group #2 to other strings
& separate group #3

7

#4 #1 #2

#3

Loop group #3 around other
strings about 6 times or until
you reach desired length

8

#4

#1 #2 #3

Add group #3 to other strings & separate group #4

9 Loop group #4 around other strings about 6 times or until you reach desired length

#4

#1 #2 #3

Repeat steps 2–9 until your bracelet is long enough!

Follow steps from page 3 to finish!

Wheee! 'Round and 'round we go!

5
BUTTERFLY

WORKS BEST WITH:
Lanyard String, Paracord

GATHER:
Two colors (one string of each for two total)
Measure and cut each string to 24–30 inches
(Note: Paracord is bulkier, so you will
need more length—36–40 inches!)

1

Tie strings together with **overhand knot** 4–5 inches from top

Secure with binder clip to keep strings from sliding

#2 #1

2

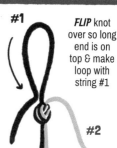

#1

FLIP knot over so long end is on top & make loop with string #1

#2

3

Wrap string #2 around loop as shown (pinch loop with your thumb & pointer finger to keep in place)

#1

#2

4

Tighten & make second loop with string #2

#1

#2

5

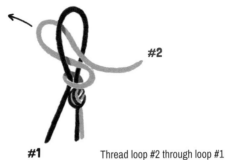

#2

#1

Thread loop #2 through loop #1

6

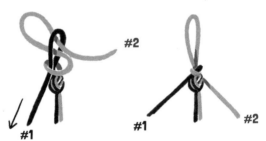

#2

#1

#1

#2

Pull long end of string #1 down
to tighten around loop #2

7

#1

#2

Make another loop with string #1

8

Thread loop #1 through loop #2

9

Pull long end of string #2 down to tighten around loop #1

Repeat steps 2–9 until your bracelet is long enough

10

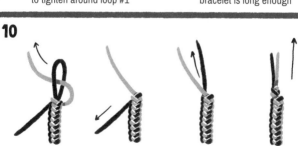

Thread working string through last loop, then tie both loose ends with **overhand knot** to finish!

6

BOX

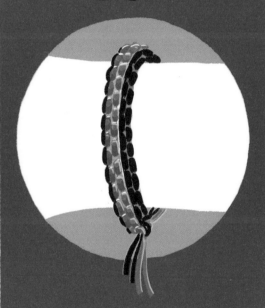

WORKS BEST WITH:
Lanyard String

GATHER:
Two colors (one string of each for two total)
Measure and cut each string to 30–36 inches

1

TIP: This bracelet has a special starting knot.

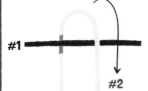

#1

#2

Place string #1 in horizontal position. Place string #2 underneath & over middle of string #1

2

#1

#2

Take right side of string #1 up & over both pieces of string #2

3

Take left piece of string #2 up & over both pieces of string #1

4

Take top piece of string #1 up & over first two pieces of string #2 & under third piece of string #2

5

#1

#4

#3

#2

Pull all four loose ends out to tighten

25

6 *TIP:* Your colors should be alternating! Make sure the crisscross pattern is on top.

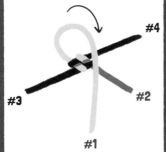

#4

#3

#2

#1

Loop string #1 up &
over to opposite side

7

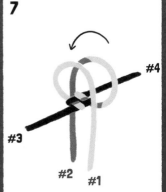

#4

#3

#2   #1

Loop string #2 up &
over to opposite side

8

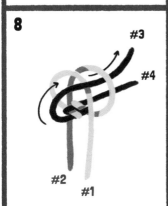

#3

#4

#2   #1

Loop string #3 up & over #1,
then weave under #2

9

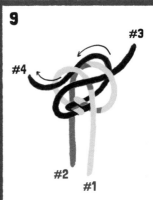

#3

#4

#2   #1

Loop string #4 up & over
#2, then weave under #1

10

#2

#3

#4

#1

Pull on all four loose ends to tighten

11

Repeat steps 6–10 until your bracelet is long enough!

Follow steps 8–10 to finish, but before you tighten, take end of each string under & up through loop to its right. Pull to tighten!

Loosen starting knot with paper clip & weave strings under it. Tighten to desired length & tie **overhand knot** as shown. Let it sit for about 30 minutes, then cut off extra string.

7
FISHTAIL

WORKS BEST WITH:
Embroidery Floss, Yarn

GATHER:
Four colors (two strings of each for eight total)
Measure and cut each string to 24–30 inches

1

Tie strings together with **overhand knot** 4–5 inches from top & secure with binder clip to keep strings from sliding

Separate strings into two groups of four, colors should be mirrored

L1
L2
LEFT L3 L4 R4 R3 **RIGHT**
R2
R1

2

Pull string L1 up & over to right group

R1
R2
L2 R3
L3 L4 **L1** R4

3

Pull string R1 up & over to left group

L2
L3 L4 **R1** **L1** R4
R2
R3

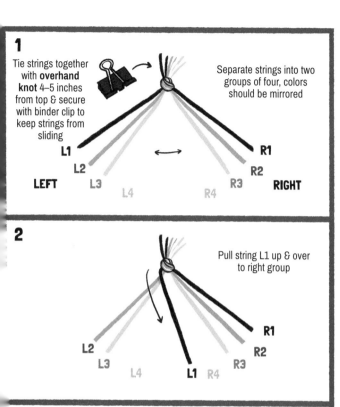

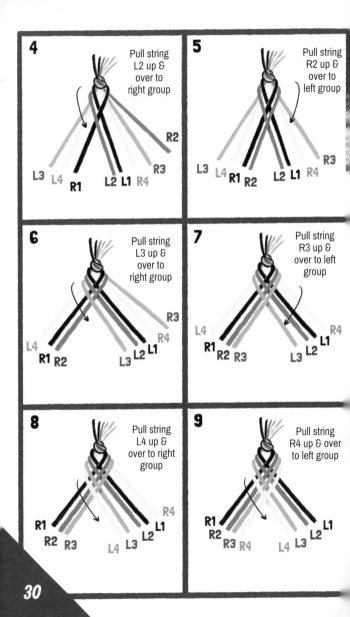

4

Pull string L2 up & over to right group

R2

L3 L4 R1 L2 L1 R4 R3

5

Pull string R2 up & over to left group

R3

L3 L4 R1 R2 L2 L1 R4

6

Pull string L3 up & over to right group

R3

R4

L4 R1 R2 L3 L2 L1

7

Pull string R3 up & over to left group

L4 R4

R1 R2 R3 L3 L2 L1

8

Pull string L4 up & over to right group

R4

R1 R2 R3 L4 L3 L2 L1

9

Pull string R4 up & over to left group

R1 R2 R3 R4 L4 L3 L2 L1

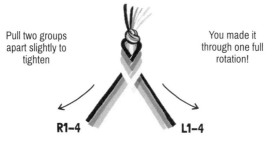

Pull two groups apart slightly to tighten

You made it through one full rotation!

R1–4 **L1–4**

Repeat steps 2–10 until your bracelet is long enough!

Follow steps from page 3 to finish!

8
DIAGONAL

WORKS BEST WITH:
Embroidery Floss, Yarn

GATHER:
Up to six colors and six total strings
Measure and cut each string to 24–30 inches

1

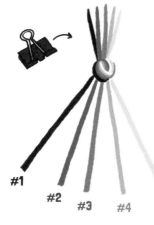

Tie strings together with **overhand knot** 4–5 inches from top & secure with binder clip to keep strings from sliding

#1　**#2**　**#3**　**#4**　**#5**　#6

Separate each string

2

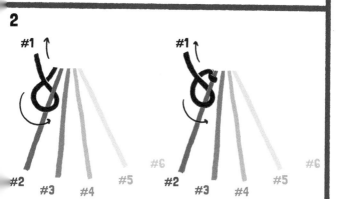

Make two **forward knots** with string #1 around string #2

Tighten each knot as you finish it

33

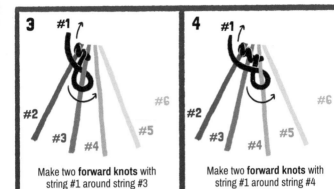

3 Make two **forward knots** with string #1 around string #3

4 Make two **forward knots** with string #1 around string #4

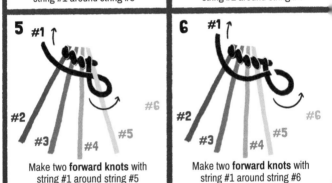

5 Make two **forward knots** with string #1 around string #5

6 Make two **forward knots** with string #1 around string #6

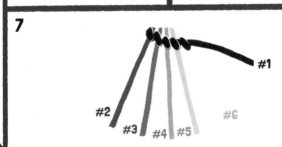

7 Tighten & set string #1 aside

8

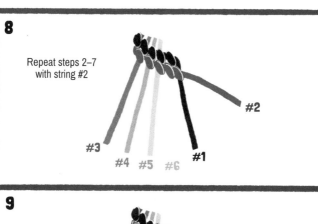

Repeat steps 2–7 with string #2

#2

#3

#4 #5 #6 #1

9

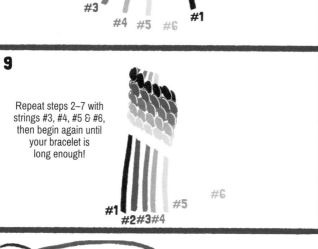

Repeat steps 2–7 with strings #3, #4, #5 & #6, then begin again until your bracelet is long enough!

#1 #2 #3 #4 #5 #6

TIP! Experiment! Try this one with different colors for a rainbow effect, or use multiple shades of the same color!

9
CHEVRON

WORKS BEST WITH:
Embroidery Floss, Yarn

GATHER:
Up to four colors (two strings of each for eight total)
Measure and cut each string to 30–36 inches

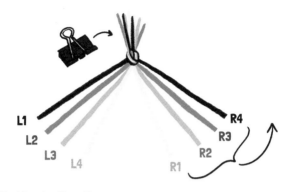

L1
L2
L3
L4

R4
R3
R2
R1

Tie strings together with **overhand knot** 4–5 inches from top & secure with binder clip to keep strings from sliding

Separate strings into two groups of four; colors should be mirrored (set aside right group)

L1

L2
L3
L4

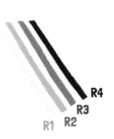

R4
R3
R2
R1

Make two **forward knots** with string L1 around string L2

Tighten each knot as you finish it

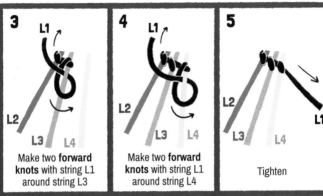

3 Make two **forward knots** with string L1 around string L3

4 Make two **forward knots** with string L1 around string L4

5 Tighten

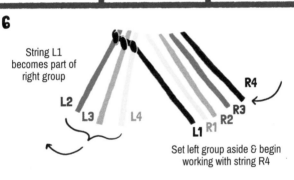

6 String L1 becomes part of right group

Set left group aside & begin working with string R4

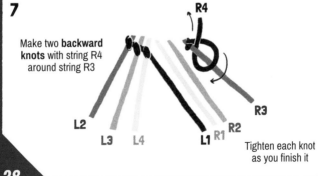

7 Make two **backward knots** with string R4 around string R3

Tighten each knot as you finish it

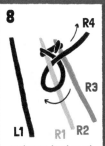

8

Make two **backward knots** with string R4 around string R2

9

Make two **backward knots** with string R4 around string R1

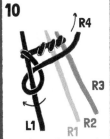

10

Make two **backward knots** with string R4 around string L1

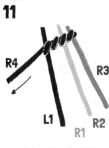

11

Tighten & string R4 becomes part of left group

12

Set right group aside & begin working with string L2

Repeat steps 2–11 until your bracelet is long enough! Follow steps from page 3 to finish!

Pretty neat, huh?

10

BRAID

WORKS BEST WITH:
Embroidery Floss, Yarn

GATHER:
Three colors (three strings of each for nine total)
Measure and cut each string to 32–36 inches

1

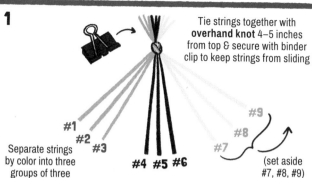

Tie strings together with **overhand knot** 4–5 inches from top & secure with binder clip to keep strings from sliding

#1
#2
#3

#9
#8
#7

Separate strings by color into three groups of three

#4 #5 #6

(set aside #7, #8, #9)

2

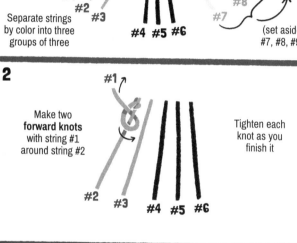

#1

Make two **forward knots** with string #1 around string #2

Tighten each knot as you finish it

#2
#3 #4 #5 #6

3

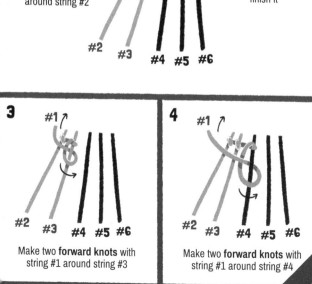

#1

#2 #3 #4 #5 #6

Make two **forward knots** with string #1 around string #3

4

#1

#2 #3 #4 #5 #6

Make two **forward knots** with string #1 around string #4

5

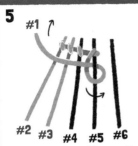

Make two **forward knots** with string #1 around string #5

6

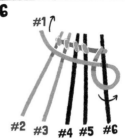

Make two **forward knots** with string #1 around string #6 (this makes five knots)

7

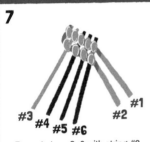

Repeat steps 2–6 with string #2, but stop just before string #1 (this makes four knots)

8

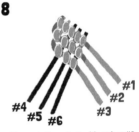

Repeat steps 2–6 with string #3, but stop just before string #2 (this makes three knots)

It should look like this:

Strings #3, #2 & #1 are now in the middle!

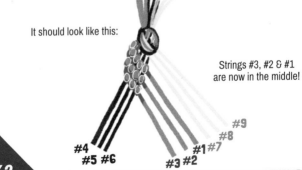

9

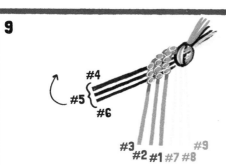

Set aside left group with strings #4, #5 & #6
& begin working with string #9

10

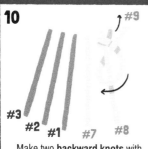

Make two **backward knots** with
string #9 around string #8 &
tighten each knot as you finish it

11

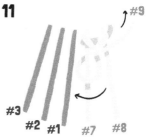

Make two **backward knots** with
string #9 around string #7

12

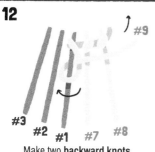

Make two **backward knots**
with string #9 around string #1

13

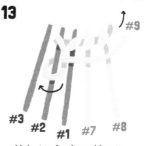

Make two **backward knots**
with string #9 around string #2

43

14

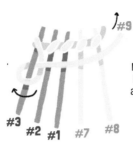

Make two **backward knots** with string #9 around string #3 (this makes five knots)

#3 #2 #1 #7 #8

15

#9
#8

#3 #2 #1 #7

Repeat steps 10–14 with string #8, but stop just before string #9 (this makes four knots)

16

#9
#8
#7

#3 #2 #1

Repeat steps 10–14 with string #7, but stop just before string #8 (this makes three knots)

It should look like this:

Strings #9, #8 & #7 are now in the middle!

#4
#5
#6 #9 #8 #7   #3 #2   #1

17

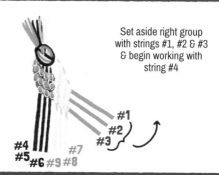

Set aside right group with strings #1, #2 & #3 & begin working with string #4

#1
#2
#3

#4
#5
#6 #7
#9 #8

18

Repeat steps 2–6 with string #4 & so on . . .

Keep going until your bracelet is long enough!

Follow steps from page 3 to finish!

It's tricky, but you'll get it in no time—you're a PRO now!

TIPS

USE DIFFERENT TYPES OF STRING!

Any of the following materials can be used for making bracelets, although some will be better suited for certain designs. They can all be found at your local craft store or online.

- *EMBROIDERY FLOSS*
- *LANYARD STRING*
- *HEMP*
- *PARACORD*
- *YARN*

EXPERIMENT!

- Explore by using different colors of string and adding more rows of each into a design.
- Try adding BEADS or BUTTONS to your bracelets!
- The patterns in this book can be tweaked to make key chains, rings, ankle bracelets, and even earrings!

PRO TIP: Instead of tape or a binder clip, try using a clipboard or a loom to keep your strings in place!

FUN FACT:

When you give a bracelet to a friend, tell them to make a wish! Friendship bracelets are meant to be worn until they fall off—when they do, your wish is said to come true!

An imprint of Macmillan Publishing Group, LLC
120 Broadway, New York, NY 10271
OddDot.com

Text and illustrations copyright © 2020 by Keith Zoo

Library of Congress Cataloging-in-Publication Data is available.
ISBN 978-1-250-24996-8

Editor: Justin Krasner
Cover designer: Colleen AF Venable & Tim Hall
Interior designer: Colleen AF Venable

Our books may be purchased in bulk for promotional,
educational, or business use. Please contact your local bookseller
or the Macmillan Corporate and Premium Sales Department at
(800) 221-7945 ext. 5442 or by email at
MacmillanSpecialMarkets@macmillan.com.

Show-How Guides is a trademark of Odd Dot.
Printed in China by Hung Hing Off-set Printing Co. Ltd.,
Heshan City, Guangdong Province
First edition, 2020

10 9 8 7 6 5 4 3 2 1

Keith Zoo

is an artist and illustrator
living in Massachusetts. You
can find more of his work
at keithzoo.com and on
Instagram @keithzoo.